Spanish Conversation templates

Ana M. Díaz-Collazos, 2025
Speech Of my Land LLC
ISBN: 979-8-9992821-9-4
Email me for updates adiazcoll@gm

I0191232

CONVERSATIONS

1. Sound Spanish out

- ca ce ci co cu /ka se si ko ku/
- ga ge gi go gu /ga he hi go gu/
- que qui /ke ki/
- gue gui /ge gi/
- ja je ji jo ju /ha he hi ho hu/
- lla lle lli llo llu AND ya ye yi yo yu (pronounce like the English J)
- ha he hi ho hu (the H shouldn't sound) /a e i o u/
- ña ñe ñi ño ñu /nya, nye, nyi, nyo, nyu/ (like you're congested or have runny nose)
- va ve vi vo vu AND ba be bi bo bu (both sound B) /ba be bi bo bu/

rra rre rri rro rru, here is where you roll the tongue. In the middle of the word written with a single R it's way softer, a bit like a soft T from American English PERA (=pear).

2. Introduce yourself

A: Hola.
B: Hola.
A: ¿Cómo te llamas?
B: Me llamo _____ (add name). ¿Y tú?
A: Me llamo _____. Mucho gusto (=much pleassure)
B: Mucho gusto.

3. Discuss meaning

A: ¿Qué significa _____?
B: Significa _____.
A: ¿Cómo se dice _____?
B: Se dice _____.

Words: luna=moon, estrella=star, sol=sun, pescador=fisherman, pescadora=fisherwoman, playa=beach, tambor=drum, vender=to sell, amor=love, fiesta=party, amiga=friend (female), amigo=friend (male)

4. Class directions

- Levanten la mano (=raise your hands), from levantar=to raise
- Levantense (=get up, everybody)
- Tomen asiento (=take a seat, everybody), from tomar=to take
- Repita (=repeat just you, please), repitan (=repeat, everybody, please), from repetir=to repeat
- Hagan un círculo (=make a circle, everybody), from hacer=to do
- Vaya al tablero (=go to the board, you alone), vayan al tablero (=go to the board, everybody)
- Escriban (=write, everybody), from escribir=to write

These verbs have an unusual conjugation where -AR ending changes to -EN to make a plural command, and -IR or -ER changes to -AN.

5. Discuss origins

A: ¿De dónde eres?
B: Yo soy de _____ (add city and state).
A: ¿De dónde son tu papá y tu mamá?
B: Ellos son de _____ (add city and state). OR: Mi papá es de _____ y mi mamá es de _____.
A: ¿De dónde es tu mejor amigo (=your best male friend) OR tu mejor amiga (=your best female friend)?
B: Él OR ella es de _____.
A: ¿De dónde es tu profesor (=your male teacher) OR tu profesora (=your female teacher) de español?
B: Él OR ella es de _____.

6. Tell your languages

A: ¿Hablas español? (=Do you speak Spanish)
B: Sí, hablo español. (=Yes, I speak Spanish) / No, no hablo español. (No, I don't speak Spanish)
A: ¿Hablas inglés? (=Do you speak English?)
B: Sí, hablo inglés. (=Yes, I speak English) / No, no hablo español. (No, I don't speak English)

7. Discuss your occupation

A: ¿En qué trabajas? (=What you-work in?)
B: Trabajo en _____ (add occupation). ¿Y tú?
A: Trabajo en _____.
Occupations: construcción (=construction), finanzas (=finance), educación (=educación), casa (=house, housework), cuidado infantil (=child care), negocios (=business), jardinería (=gardening), ingeniería (=engeneering), ventas (=sells), comida (=food). OR:
Soy estudiante (instead of "trabajo en").

If you are retired, respond:
Trabajé en _____, pero estoy pensionado (male) OR pensionada (female).

8. Discuss your major

A: ¿Qué estudias? (=What do you study?)
B: Estudio _____ (add major). ¿Y tú?
A: Estudio _____.

Tip: Try to find the easiest translation to your major. Adapt it to one word.

- Arte /ár-teh/ = art (studio)
- Bioquímica /bee-oh-kee-mee-kah/ = biochemistry
- Ciencia política /syen-syah poh-lee-tee-kah/ = political science
- Ciencias de la salud /syen-syahs deh lah sah-lood/ = health sciences
- Computación /kom-poo-tah-syón/ = computer science
- Contaduría /kon-tah-doo-ree-ah/ = accounting
- Criminología /kree-mee-no-loh-hee-ah/ = criminology
- Deportes /deh-pór-tehs/ = sports
- Deportes extremos /deh-pór-tehs eks-treh-mohs/ = adventure or extreme sports
- Ecología /eh-koh-loh-hee-ah/ = environmental studies
- Economía /eh-koh-no-mee-ah/ = economics
- Educación /eh-doo-kah-syón/ = Education
- Geología /heh-oh-loh-hee-ah/ = geology
- Historia /ees-toh-ree-ah/ = history

- Ingeniería /een-heh-neh-ree-ah/ = engineering
- Lenguas /léng-wahs/ = languages
- Matemática /mah-teh-má-tee-kah/ = math
- Música /moo-see-kah/ = music
- Negocios /neh-gó-syohs/ = business
- Nutrición /noo-tree-syón/ = nutrition
- Periodismo /peh-ree-oh-dees-moh/ = journalism
- Psicología /see-koh-loh-hee-ah/ = psychology
- Salud pública /sah-lood poob-lee-kah/ = public health
- Secundaria /seh-koon-dah-ree-ah/ = middle school or high school
- Sociología /soh-syoh-loh-hee-ah/ = Sociology

9. Tell why you practice Spanish

A: ¿Por qué estudias español? (=Why you-study Spanish)
B: Estudio (=I-study) español porque _____.
Reasons: Me gusta (=I like it), Voy a viajar (=I'm going to travel), Es importante para mi trabajo (=It's important for my job), and/or explain in English.

10.   Add your contacts

A: ¿Cuál es tu teléfono?
B: Es ___ (_____), ___ (_____), ___ (_____), ___ (_____), ___ (_____), ___ (_____), ___ (_____),___ (_____), ___ (_____),
(Write it in numbers, then add the number in words).
A: ¿Cómo te llamas?
B: Me llamo _____.
A: ¿Cómo se escribe? (=how is it written?)
B:
Se escribe ___ (_____), ___ (_____), ___ (_____), ___ (_____), ___ (_____), ___ (_____), ___ (_____),___ (_____), ___ (_____),
(Write the letter, then the way it is pronounced)

1 (uno), 2 (dos), 3 (tres), 4 (cuatro), 5 (cinco), 6 (seis), 7 (siete), 8 (ocho), 9 (nueve), 10 (diez), 11 (once), 12 (doce), 13 (trece), 14 (catorce), 15 (quince), 20 (veinte), 30 (treinta), 40 (cuarenta), 45 (cuarenta y cinco), 50 (cincuenta), 60 (sesenta), 70 (setenta), 80 (ochenta), 90 (noventa), 100 (cien)

ABC:
A (ah) B (be) C (se) CH (che) D (de) E (eh) F (efe) G (he), H (ache), I (ee) J (hota) K (ka) L (ele) LL (eye) M (eme) N (ene) Ñ (enie) O (oh) P (pe) Q (ku) R (ere) S (ese) T (te) U (oo) V (ube) W (doble be) X (equis) Y (i griega) Z (seta)

11.   Repond "no" to habits

bailar=to dance
A: ¿_____? = do you dance?
B: **No, no _____.** = no, I don't dance
Limpiar la casa=to clean the house
A: ¿_____ **la casa?** =do you clean the house
B: **No, yo no _____ la casa.**=no, I don't clean the house
manejar=to drive
A: ¿_____? =do you drive?
B: No, yo no _____.=no, I don't drive
fumar=to smoke
A: ¿_____? =do you smoke?
B: **No, yo no _____.**=no, I don't smoke
trabajar=to work
A: ¿_____? =do you work?
B: **No, yo no _____.**=no, I don't work
mirar televisión=watch TV
A: ¿_____? =do you watch TV?
B: **No, yo no _____.**=no, I don't watch TV

Conjugate in the present indicative:
To dance, bailar=(tú, you) bail**as**, (yo, I) bail**o**
Say yes: Sí, yo _____.

12.   What you usually eat

A: ¿Qué comes en el <u>desayuno</u>? (=What do you eat for breakfast?)
B: Yo como _____. (=I eat …)
A: ¿Qué tomas en el <u>desayuno</u>? (=What do you drink for breakfast?)
B: Yo tomo _____. (=I drink …)

<u>Breakfast things</u>: Nada=nothing, huevos=eggs, pan=bread, queso=cheese, salchicha=saussage, fruta=fruit, cereal=cereal, café=coffee, leche=milk, agua=wáter, jugo=juice

almuerzo (lunch), cena (dinner) OR comida (food, dinner)

13. Discuss your routines

A: ¿Trabajas todos los días?
B: Sí, yo _____. / No, yo no _____.

<u>Verbs</u>: caminar (=to walk), dibujar (=to draw), trabajar (=to work), descansar (=to rest), bailar (=to dance), manejar (=to drive), estudiar (=to study), practicar deportes (=to practice sports), cocinar (=to cook), disparar (=to shoot), montar bicicleta (=to ride a bike), correr (=to run), barrer (=to sweep), tejer (=to knit), coser (=to sew)

<u>Conjugate in the present indicative:</u>
To dance, bail~~ar~~=(tú, you) bail**as**, (yo, I) bail**o**
To sweep, barr~~er~~=(tú, you) barr**es**, (yo, I) barr**o**

14. Discuss your partner's routines

C: ¿Él OR Ella trabaja todos los días?
A: Sí, él OR ella trabaja todos los días. (Referring to B)

<u>Conjugate in the él or ella form</u>: Just delete the R

15. Tell expected time for your plans

A: ¿Cuándo vas a descansar (=to rest)?
B: Voy a descansar _____.
(add time expression).
A: ¿Cuándo vas a comer (=to eat)?
B: Voy a comer _____
A: ¿Cuándo vas a regresar a tu casa (=to return home)?
B: Voy a regresar a casa _____.
A: ¿Cuándo vas a hacer la tarea de español (=to do the Spanish homework)?
B: Voy a hacer la tarea de español _____.

<u>Time expressions</u>: mañana (tomorrow), más tarde (later), por la noche (in the night), por la tarde (in the afternoon), por la mañana (in the morning).

16.   Tell your plans

A: ¿Qué vas a hacer mañana?=What are you going to do tomorrow?

B: Yo voy a _____, _____ y _____ mañana.

Actions: descansar (=to rest), trabajar (=to work), estudiar (=to study), viajar (=to travel), mirar television (=to watch TV), limpiar la casa (=to clean the house)

17.   Discuss someone else's plans

C: ¿Él OR Ella va a <u>descansar</u> mañana?

A: Sí, él OR ella va a descansar mañana OR No, ella no va a descansar mañana. (Referring to B)

18.   Guess your partner's plans

A: ¿Vas a _____ mañana?

B: Sí, voy a _____ mañana. OR No, no voy a _____ mañana.

Actions: descansar (=to rest), trabajar (=to work), estudiar (=to study), viajar (=to travel), mirar television (=to watch TV), limpiar la casa (=to clean the house), montar bicicleta (=to ride a bike), estudiar español (=to study Spanish).

19.   Discuss the past (AR forms)

viaja~~r~~=to travel, have a long trip

A: ¿Ayer via**jaste**? = did you travel yesterday?

B: **No, no** viaj**é** = no, I didn't travel

Sí, viaj**é** = yes, I traveled.

trabaja~~r~~=to work

A: ¿Ayer traba**jaste**? = did you travel yesterday?

B: **No, no** trabaj**é** = no, I didn't travel

Sí, trabaj**é** = yes, I traveled.

mira~~r~~ televisión=to watch TV

A: ¿Ayer mir**aste** televisión? = did you watch TV yesterday?

B: **No, no** mir**é** televisión = no, I didn't watch TV

Sí, trabaj**é** = yes, I watched TV

Other verbs you can use ending in AR: limpiar (to clean), manejar (to drive), lavar (to wash), cocinar (to cook), pasear (to stroll), hablar por teléfono (to talk over the phone)

20.   Discuss someone else's past

C: ¿Él OR ella _____ ayer (=yesterday)?
A: Sí, él OR ella _____ ayer.

Make the third person: delete the -AR and add -Ó with stress.

21.   Discuss the past (ER, IR forms)

barrer=to sweep
A: ¿Ayer barr**iste**? = did you sweep yesterday?
B: **No, no** barr**í** = no, I didn't sweep
Sí, barr**í** = Yes, I sweeped.
correr=to run
A: ¿Ayer corr**iste**? = did you run yesterday?
B: **No, no** corr**í** = no, I didn't run
Sí, corr**í** = Yes, I ran
comer = to eat
A: ¿Ayer com**iste** tamales? = did you eat tamales yesterday?
B: **No, no** com**í** tamales = no, I didn't eat
Sí, com**í** tamales = Yes, I ran
Other verbs you can use ending in ER: leer (to read), salir (to go out), escribir emails (write emails)

22.   Discuss someone else's past IR and ER forms

C: ¿Él OR ella _____ ayer (=yesterday)?
A: Sí, él OR ella _____ ayer.

Make the third person: delete the -ER or -IR and add -IÓ with stress.

23.   Discuss your childhood routines

A: ¿Qué hacías los domingos por la mañana cuando eras niño OR niña?
B: Cuando yo era niño OR niña, yo _____.

Imperfects
   • mirar Televisión (=watch TV) – imperfect: **miraba**

- jugar con (=play with) – imperfect: **jugaba**
- montar bicicleta (=to ride a bike) – imperfect: **montaba**
- pintar (=to pain) – imperfect: **pintaba**
- dormir (=to sleep) – imperfect: **dormía**
- salir (=to go out) – imperfect: **salía**

24.   Discuss how you cope with pain

A: ¿Qué haces cuando te duele _____ (=what do you do when it hurts + part of body)?
B: Cuando me duele _____ (=when it hurts + part of the body), yo _____ (add action conjugated in the yo-form).

Parts of the body: te duele la cabeza (=head), te duele el pecho (=chest), te duele la espalda (=back), te duelen las piernas (=legs), te duelen las manos (=hands)

Verbs: llamar al doctor=call the doctor, practicar deportes=practice sports, tomar medicina=take a medicine, comer=to eat, descansar=to rest, llorar=to cry, aplicar hielo=apply ice

conjugate in the yo-form: delete the AR part, and add O.

25.   Borrow something

A: ¿Tienes _____? (Do you have + item)
B: Sí, tengo / No, no tengo. (Yes, I have / No, I don't have)
A: ¿Me ____ prestas? (Do you lend it to me?)
B: Sí, con mucho gusto te ____ presto. (Yes, I lend it to you with pleasure)

Object Pronouns:
it=**lo** cuaderno (notebook), teléfono (phone), papel (paper), libro (book), lápiz (pencil), cargador (charger), borrador (eraser), computador (computer)
it=**la** cinta (tape), regla (ruler), computadora (computer), mascarilla (face mask)
them=**las** tijeras (scissors), gafas (glasses)
them=**los** audífonos (headphones), marcadores (markers)

26.   Express what you want

A: ¿Quieres _____? (do you want)
B: Sí, quiero _____ / No, no quiero _____.

Verbs: rezar (to pray), limpiar la casa (to clean the house), correr (to run), beber (to drink), lavar los platos (to wash the dishes) , montar bicicleta (to ride bike), montar caballo (to ride horse), sacar al perro (take the dog out)

27.   Describe yourself

A: ¿Cómo eres?
B: Yo soy _____, _____ y _____. ¿Y tú?
A: Yo soy _____, _____ y _____.

- Moreno (male) /morena (female) = darker skin
- Blanco (male) / blanca (female) = light skin
- Alto (male) / alta (female) = tall
- Bajo (male) / baja (female) = short
- Mediano (male) / mediana (female) = middle size
- Gordito (male) / gordita (female) = chubby
- Flaco (male) / flaca (female) = skinny
- Bonita=pretty (only woman)
- Guapa=beautiful (woman)
- Guapo, pintoso=handsome (man)
- Hermoso OR hermosa=gorgeous
- Feo OR fea=ugly
- Feíto OR feíta=ugly, but sweet
- Lindo OR linda=sweet

28.   Describe hair color and eyes

A: ¿Cómo eres?
B: Yo tengo ojos (=eyes) _____ (adjetivo) y pelo (=hair) _____ (=adjetivo of color), _____ (=adjetivo of texture) y _____ (=adjetivo of lenght).
B: Yo tengo ojos (=eyes) _____ (adjetivo) y pelo (=hair) _____ (=adjetivo of color), _____ (=adjetivo of texture) y _____ (=adjetivo of lenght).

Hair color: Verde=green, Azul=blue, Rojo=red, Café OR castaño=Brown, Blanco=white, Negro=black, Rubio=blonde

Hair texture: Crespo=curly, Liso=straight, Ondulado=wavy

Hair size: Largo=long, corto=short

Eyes color: Verdes=green, Azules=blue, Cafés =Brown, Negros=black

29.   Describe a friend or family member

A: ¿Cómo se llama tu amigo OR amiga?
B: Se llama _____ (add name).
A: ¿Cómo es?
B: Es _____ y _____. Tiene pelo
_____, _____ y _____. Tiene ojos
_____ y _____.

Family members: tu papá (=your dad), tu mamá (=your mom), tu abuelo (=your grandpa), tu abuela (=your grandma), tu hijo (=your son), tu hija (=your daughter), tu hermana (=your sister), tu hermano (=your brother), tu primo (=your male cousing), tu prima (=your female cousin), tu tío (=your uncle), tu tía (=your aunt), tu suegra (=your mother in law), tu suegro (=your father in law), tu novio (=your boyfriend), tu novia (=your girlfriend), tu esposo (=your husband), tu esposa (=your wife), tu cuñado (=your brother in law), tu cuñada (=your sister in law)

30.   State where you live = vivir

A: ¿Dónde vives?
B: Yo vivo en _____ (add city and state). ¿Y tú?
A: Yo vivo en _____.

31.   Guess likes and dislikes:

A: ¿Te gusta _____?
B: Sí, me gusta _____. / No, no me gusta _____.
(pick at least four verbs)
A: ¿A tu amigo OR amiga?
B: A _____ (add name) le gusta _____.

Verbs remain in the infinitive: Caminar (=to walk), cocinar (=to cook), limpiar (=to clean), cantar (=to sing), bailar (=to dance), subir montañas (=to climb mountains), hacer deportes (=to do sports), sacar al perro (=to stroll the dog), tocar guitarra (=to play guitar), dibujar (=to draw), leer (=to read), ver television (=to watch TV)

32.   Tell likes and dislikes

A: ¿Qué te gusta hacer?
B: Me gusta _____, _____ y _____. ¿Qué te gusta hacer?
B: Me gusta _____, _____ y _____.

33.   Discuss beliefs

A: ¿Crees en _____?
B: Sí, creo en _____. / No, no creo en _____.
A: ¿En qué crees? (=In what do you believe)
B: Yo creo en _____ (add something you believe in).

Beliefs: 1) Dios, 2) la virgen, 3) los santos, 4) los orishas, 5) las vacunas, 6) el gobierno, 7) la madre tierra (=mother earth), 8) Santa Claus, 9) Big Bang, 10) Adán y Eva.

34.   Beliefs turned poetry

A: ¿Crees que _____?
B: Sí, creo que _____.

Thing / verb: Flores / hablar, Árboles / bailar, Luna / caminar, Sol / iluminar, Los animales / pensar (=piensan), Las piedras / esperar (=wait), La lluvia (=snow) / cantar, Las montañas (=mountains) / roncar (=snore), Los ríos / correr
Just delete the R and add an N

35.   School supplies

A: ¿Qué traes en tu mochila?
B: Yo _____ (add verb) _____, _____ y _____ (list items) en mi mochila. ¿Y tú?
A: Yo _____ (add verb) _____, _____ y _____ (list items) en mi mochila.

School supplies: cuaderno (=notebook), computador (=computer), lapicero (=pen), lápiz (=pencil), libro (=book), teléfono (=telephone), llaves (=keys), billetera (=wallet), tarjetas de crédito (=credit card), cinta (=tape), regla (=ruler), tijeras (=scissors), curita (=bandaid), gafas (=eyes glasses)

36.   Visa interview

A: Embassy officer, B: Visa requester
A: ¿Cómo te llamas?
B: _____. (make up Hispanic name)
A: ¿Cómo se escribe?
B: _____.
A: ¿De dónde eres?
B: _____. (find a city in Dominican Republic)
A: ¿Cuál es tu etnicidad?
B: Yo soy _____.
A: ¿Por qué vas a viajar a Estados Unidos?
B: Porque voy a _____ (add a verb in the infitive explaining reason).
A: ¿Cuándo vas a viajar?
B: _____ (add pretend date).
A: ¿Quién es tu familia?
B:_____. (List your family members)
A: ¿Dónde viven?
B:_____.
A: ¿Cuánto dinero tienes en el banco?
B: Tengo _____.
A: ¿Tienes casas?
B: _____ (add a pretend house)
A: Su visa ha sido negada (=Your visa has been denied)

37.   Framed by the police

A: ¿Qué _____ en tu mochila?
B: Yo _____ (verb traer) _____, _____ y _____ (add school supplies).
A: Necesitamos hacer **una requisa** (=a screening).
(Simulate a screening of your classmates' bag)

C: Él OR Ella _____ (verb traer) _____,
_____ y _____.
A: No es verdad, no _____ (repeat the three things you got charged with).

From Cuba out: plátano, bongos, guayabera, machete, ron, güiro, yuca, triple, polaina, lechón, figura de santo, disco de Carlos Puebla.

From Estados Unidos into Cuba: remedio (=medicine), video-juegos (=video games), disco de Celia Cruz, carteras (=purses), joyas (=jewel), mantequilla de maní (=peanut butter), diez mil dólares (=10.000 dollars)

38.   Guess occupation - escribir (to write)

Hint: Take a time to match things someone writes with certain occupation

A: ¿Qué _____ (=escribir, to write) mucho (=a lot)?
B: Yo _____ (add verb) _____ (add one thing you usually write).

Things to write: emails, textos (=text messages), ensayos (=essays), poemas (=poems), cuentos (=stories), cartas (=letters), contratos (=contracts), multas (=fines), planos (=maps, sketches), cáculos (=calculations) facturas (=bills), guiones (=scripts), código (=code)

A: ¿Por qué?
B: Porque soy _____ (add occupation).

Occupations: estudiante (=student), profesor OR profesora (=Teacher), escritor OR escritora (=writer), abogado OR abogada (=lawyer), camarero OR camarera (=waiter or waitress), guionista (=script writer), vendedor (=sale person, clerck), policía (=police officer), arquitecto (=architect), ingeniero OR ingeniera (=engineer), programador (=developer)

39. How you cope with emotions

A: ¿Qué haces cuándo estás _____ (add emotion)? = what do you do when you are (feeling) _____?
B: Cuando estoy _____ (add emotion), yo _____.
=When I am (feeling) _____, yo
_____ (add action conjugated in the YO form).

Emotions: feliz (=happy), triste (=sad), enojado OR enojada (=angry), nervioso OR nerviosa (=nervous), estresado OR estresada (=stressed), cansado OR cansada (=tired), emocionado OR emocionada (=excited), enamorado OR enamorada (=in love)

Actions: caminar (=to walk), tirar cosas (=to throw things), mirar televisión (=to watch TV), descansar (=to rest), tomar algo (=to drink something), comer chocolate (=to eat chocolate), llamar a un amigo OR amiga (=to call a friend), llorar (=to cry), gritar (=to yell), escribir (=to write).

Delete two last letters and add O

40. Frequency to do sports, homework, food

A: ¿Cuando (=when) haces deporte (=sports)?
B: Yo _____ deporte _____ (add frequency).
A: ¿Cuándo haces tareas (=homework)?
B: Yo _____ tareas (=homework) _____ .
A: ¿Cuándo haces comida (=food)?
B: Yo _____ comida _____.
A: ¿Cuándo haces oficio (=chores)?
B: Yo _____ oficio _____.

Hacer (=to do, to make) adds a G in the YO-form: Yo hago.

Frequency: todos los días (=every day), casi todos los días (=almost every day), casi siempre (=almost always), siempre (=always), a veces (=some times), rara vez (=seldom), nunca (=never), de vez en cuando (=from time to time)

41.   Tell time

A: ¿Qué horas son ahora (=right now)?
B: Son las _____ (add hour) y _____ (add minute)
de la mañana (am) / tarde (pm before 6) / noche (pm after 6).

Hour: Dos (2), tres (3), cuatro (4), cinco (5), seis (6), siete (7), ocho
(8), nueve (9), diez (10), once (11), doce (12)

But: la una (1)

Minutes: diez (10), quince OR cuarto (15), media OR treinta (30),
cuarenta (40), cuarenta y cinco (45), 50 (cincuenta)

42.   Time zones

A: ¿Qué horas son ahora (=right now) en _____ (add country)?
B: Son las _____ (add hour) y _____ (add minute)
de la mañana (am) / tarde (pm before 6) / noche (pm after 6).

Examples: España (4:30 am), Colorado (8:30pm), Hong Kong
(10:30am), India (8:30), Hawaii (6:30pm), Nigeria (3:30am), Ghana
(2:30am), Japón (11:30am)

43.   Time of your day routines

A: ¿A qué horas _____ (add verb in the tú form)?
B: Yo _____ (same verb in the yo-form) a las
_____ y _____ de la _____.

Verbs, with conjugations in yo/tú forms: desayunar (=have
breakfast) desayuno/desayunas, salir de la casa (=go out of home)
salgo/sales, almorzar (=to have lunch), almuerzo/almuerzas,
trabajar (=to work) trabajo/trabajas, regresar a la casa (=to return
home) regreso/regresas, manejar (=to drive) manejo/manejas,
cuidar niños (=take care of children) cuido/cuidas, limpiar (=to
clean) limpio/limpias

44.   Time of someone else's day routines

C: ¿A qué horas él OR ella _____?
A: Él OR ella _____ a las _____ y
_____ de la _____. (referring to B)

___

45. Time of your morning and evening routines

A: ¿A qué horas _____ (add verb in the tú form)?
B: Yo _____ (same verb in the yo-form) a las
_____ y _____ de la _____.

Reflexive verbs:
Levantarse
te levantas (=you get up) / me levanto (=I get up)
Bañarse
te bañas (=you take a shower) / me baño (=I take a shower)

Cepillarse los dientes
Te cepillas los dientes (=you brush your teeth) / me cepillo los dientes (=I brush my teeth)
Afeitarse
Te afeitas (=you shave) / me afeito (=I shave)
Maquillarse
Te maquillas (=you make up) / me maquillo (=I make up)
Cambiarse
Te cambias (=you change your clothes) / me cambio (=I change my clothes)
Acostarse
Te acuestas (=you lay down, go to bed) / me acuesto (=I lay down, go to verb)

46. Discuss ability to play an instrument

A: ¿Puedes tocar un instrumento?
B: Sí, puedo tocar _____ (add instrument). OR
No, no puedo tocar nada (=I can't play nothing).
A: ¿Qué instrumento quieres aprender a tocar?
B: Quiero aprender a tocar _____.

Instrumentos: Bongos, güiro, campana (=cowbell), maracas, guitarra (=guitar), piano, flauta, violín, arpa (=harp), trompeta (=trumpet), or add one

47.　　　Refuse an invitation

A: ¿Quieres _____ (add verb) conmigo (=with me)?
B: Sí, quiero, pero no puedo porque _____.

Verbs: bailar (=to dance), salir (=to go out), comer (=to eat), hacer deportes (=to do sports), montar bicicleta (=to bike), montar caballo (=to ride a horse), jugar video-juegos (=play video-games)

Phrases that add reasons: tengo tarea (=I have homework), no sé bailar (=I don't know how to dance), estoy enfermo OR enferma (=I'm sick), tengo una reunión (=I have a meeting), estoy dejando la bebida (=I'm quitting the drink).

48.　　　Ongoing actions

A: ¿Qué estás haciendo?
B: Estoy _____, _____, y _____.
A: ¡Ay que bueno! ¿Puedo acompañarte?
B: ¡Si, por supuesto!

Ejemplos: caminado (walking), haciendo tarea (doing homework), comiendo (eating), hablando por teléfono (talking on the pone), tomando café (drinking coffee) , montando caballo (riding a horse), haciendo ejercicio (doing exercise), limpiando la casa (cleaning the house), escuchando a música (listening to music)

49.　　　Describe personality

A: ¿Cómo eres en tu personalidad?
B: Yo soy _____, _____ y _____.
A: ¿Cómo es tu _____ (add amigo OR amiga with name, OR family member)?
B: Ella OR Él es _____, _____ y _____.

Adjetivos de personalidad: Malgeniado or malgeniada (=bad mood), agradable (=nice), sencillo or sencilla (=simple, humble), mentiroso or mentirosa (=lier), tímido or tímida, extrovertido or extrovertida, perezoso or perezosa (=lazy), trabajador or trabajadora (=hard worker), fiestero or fiestera (=party goer), comelón or comelona (=eater), celoso or celosa (=jelous), creído or creída (=snobby), chistoso or chistosa (=fun, silly), peleón or peleona (=fight seeker), hablador or habladora (=talkative), resabiado or resabiada (=picky eater), tranquilo or tranquila, gritón or gritona (=yeller), nervioso or nerviosa

50.   Routines with harder verbs

A: ¿A qué horas _____ (volver, to return) a la casa?
B: Yo _____ (volver, to return) a la casa a las
_____ (hour) de la tarde OR noche.
A: ¿A qué horas te _____ (dormir, to sleep)?
B: Yo me _____ (dormir, to sleep) a las
_____ (hour) de la noche.

O changes to UE

51.   Talk about opinions

A: ¿Qué _____ (pensar, to think in the tú form, E changes to
IE) de _____ (add restaurant in your town)?
B: Yo _____ (pensar, to think in the yo form) que es bueno
OR malo.

52.   Tell hard emotions

A: ¿Cómo estás?
B: Estoy _____.
Confundir (=to confuse) -> confudido OR confundida
Enojar (=to make angry) -> enojado OR enojada
Deprimir (=to depress) -> _____.
Frustrar (=to frustrate) -> _____.
Sorprender (=to surprise) -> _____.
Preocupar (=to worry) -> _____.
Decepcionar (=to disappoint) -> _____.
Cansar (=to tire) -> _____.

53.   Whether you have done weird things

Cazar (=to hunt)
A: ¿Alguna vez ____ _____ un animal?
B: No, nunca ____ _____ comida cruda.
Sí, una vez / dos veces / varias veces

Cometer (=to commit)
A: ¿Alguna vez ____ _____ un delito (=crime)?
B: No, nunca ____ _____ un delito.
Sí, una vez / dos veces / varias veces.

Probar (=to taste)
A: ¿Alguna vez ____ _____ mocos (=boggers)?
B: No, nunca ____ _____ mocos.
Sí, una vez / dos veces / varias veces.

Tener (=to hunt)
A: ¿Alguna vez ____ _____ COVID?
B: No, nunca ____ _____ COVID.
Sí, una vez / dos veces / varias veces

Pelear (=to fight)
A: ¿Alguna vez ____ _____ a puños (=to fists)?
B: No, nunca ____ _____ a puños.
Sí, una vez / dos veces / varias veces.

Estar (=to be located)
A: ¿Alguna vez ____ _____ en el hospital?
B: No, nunca ____ _____ en el hospital.
Sí, una vez / dos veces / varias veces

Llamar (=to call)
A: ¿Alguna vez ____ _____ a la policía?
B: No, nunca ____ _____ a la policía.
Sí, una vez / dos veces / varias veces.

Viajar (=to travel)
A: ¿Alguna vez ____ _____ a un país hispano?
B: No, nunca ____ _____ a un país hispano.
Sí, una vez / dos veces / varias veces.

Acariciar (=to caress, to touch)
A: ¿Alguna vez ____ _____ una serpiente?
B: No, nunca ____ _____ una serpiente.
Sí, una vez / dos veces / varias veces

Comer (=to eat)
A: ¿Alguna vez _____ _____ insectos?
B: No, nunca _____ _____ insectos.
Sí, una vez / dos veces / varias veces.

Ver (=to see) VISTO
A: ¿Alguna vez _____ _____ un platillo volador (=flying saucer)?
B: No, nunca _____ _____ un platillo volador (=flying saucer).
Sí, una vez / dos veces / varias veces.

Hacer (=to do) HECHO
A: ¿Alguna vez _____ _____ el ridículo?
B: No, nunca _____ _____ el ridículo.
Sí, una vez / dos veces / varias veces.

54.   Discuss clothes

A: ¿Qué llevas puesto? (=What do you bring put-on?)
B: Llevo puesto _____, _____ y
_____. ¿Y tú?
A: Llevo puesto _____, _____ y
_____.

Clothing: sombrero (=hat), camiseta (=T-shirt), gorra (=cap), saco (=coat, jacket), vaqueros (=jeans), sandalias (=sandals), tacones (=high heles), falda (=skirt), pantalones (=pants), corbata (=tie), blusa (=blouse), botas (=boots)

55.   Order at a restaurant

A: ¿Cuánto cuesta la gringa? (=How much is _____?
B: Cuesta _____ dólares.
A: ¿Qué lleva? (=What does it bring, referring to ingredients)
B: Lleva _____, _____ y _____.
A: **Deme** _____ gringas. (=Give me # gringas)
B: Sí, con mucho gusto. ¿Qué carne (=meet) quiere?
A: Quiero _____.

Options: **carne asada**, **pollo** (=chicken), **carnitas** (=pork strips), **sin carne** (=without meet)

B: ¿Tortillas de harina (=wheat) o de maíz (=corn)?

A: De _____ (pick one).
B: ¿Y de beber?
A: **Deme** _____. (=Give me)
B: ¿Algo más? (=Anything else?)
A: _____ (improvise).

Options: cerveza (=beer), margarita (=daisy), agua (=water), gaseosa (=soda), limonada

Do all discussion with other dishes: tacos, enchiladas, burritos, fajitas, sopa

56.   Bargain at a street market

A: ¿Tiene _____? (=do you have)
B: Sí, tengo _____ (=yes, I have)
A: ¿Cuánto cuesta? (=how much does it cost)
B: Cuesta _____ (add prize).
A: ¿Me lo OR la puede vender a _____ (add proposed prize)?
B: Sí, puedo OR No, no puedo.

Ítems: papa (=potatoe), tomate (=tomatoe), cebolla (=onion), aguacate (=avocado), pimiento (=pepper), naranja (=orange), carne (=meat), pollo (=chicken), pescado (=fish), calabaza (=pumpkin), manzana (=apple)

57.   Nationalities

A: ¿De dónde es _____ (add artist)?
B: Es de _____ (add country).
A: ¿Cuál es **su** (=his/her) nacionalidad?
B: Es _____.

Repeat the whole conversation until adding all artists.
Nationalities: argentino o argentina, boricua (from Puerto Rico), boliviano o boliviana, brasilero o brasilera, chileno o chilena, colombiano o colombiana, costarricense OR tico / tica, cubano o cubana, dominicano o dominicana, ecuatoriano o ecuatoriana, estadounidense OR gringo / gringa, español o española (from Spain), mexicano o mexicana, peruano o peruana, nicaragüense OR nica, panameño o panameña, venezolano o venezolana

- Bad Bunny es de Puerto Rico
- Taíno es de Puerto Rico
- Daddy Yankee es de Puerto Rico
- Gaby es de Panamá
- Becky G es de Republica Dominicana
- Carol G es de Colombia
- Mau y Ricky son de Venezuela
- Arcángel es de República Dominicana
- Maluma es de Colombia
- JLo es de Estados Unidos
- Rosalía es de España

58.   Locate countries in a map

A: ¿Dónde está _____ (add country)?
B: Está en _____ (add continent).

Norteamérica = Estados Unidos, Canadá, México
Centroamérica = Guatemala, Belice, Honduras, El Salvador, Nicaragua, Costa Rica, Panamá

Caribe = Cuba, República Dominicana, Haití, Jamaica, Trinidad y Tobago, Bahamas, Barbados, San Vicente y las Granadinas, Santa Lucía, Dominica, Antigua y Barbuda, San Cristóbal y Nieves, Granada

Sudamérica = Colombia, Venezuela, Ecuador, Perú, Bolivia, Brasil, Paraguay, Chile, Argentina, Uruguay

Europa = España, Francia, Alemania, Italia, Reino Unido, Portugal, Países Bajos, Bélgica, Suiza, Austria, Polonia, Noruega, Suecia, Finlandia, Dinamarca, Irlanda, Grecia, Hungría, Rumanía, Ucrania, Rusia

África = Egipto, Nigeria, Sudáfrica, Kenia, Etiopía, Marruecos, Argelia, Ghana, Senegal, Angola, Tanzania, Túnez, Mozambique, Sudán, República Democrática del Congo

Asia = China, India, Japón, Corea del Sur, Indonesia, Vietnam,

Tailandia, Filipinas, Arabia Saudita, Irán, Irak, Turquía, Israel, Pakistán, Malasia, Siria, Catar

Oceanía = Australia, Nueva Zelanda, Papúa Nueva Guinea, Fiyi, Samoa, Tonga, Islas Salomón, Vanuatu

59.   Discuss someone's expectations on "me"

"Yo soy tu mamá. Yo tengo muchas expectativas sobre ti. En el futuro, tú vas a ganar mucho dinero, hacer muchos negocios importantes, tener fama, comprar una mansión, te vas a casar, nunca te vas a divorciar, vas a tener tres hijos, salir de Estados Unidos, vivir en Europa, y luego vas a volver a vivir conmigo".

Mi mamá quiere que yo _____ (add verb in subjunctive). (Create at least 5 sentences)

Verbs conjugated infinitive -> subjunctive: hacer -> haga, tener -> tenga, comprar -> compre, casar -> case, divorciar -> divorcie, salir -> salga, vivir -> viva, volver -> vuelva

Subjunctive: 1) take the yo-form gano (ganar, to win), 2) delete the ending gan, 2) change A to E and E/I to A, according to the verb gane (YO and Él subjunctive forms)

60.   What you were doing

Think about something you were doing just right before this moment, and ask each other:

A: ¿Qué estabas haciendo?
B: Estaba _____. ¿Y tú?
A: Estaba _____.

To make the NDO form: delete -AR and add -ANDO, delete -ER and -IR and add -IENDO

Verbs: manejar (=to drive), estudiar (=study), hablar por teléfono (=to talk over the phone), pensar (=to think), ver tiktoks (=to watch tiktoks)

61.   Places you were around yesterday

A: ¿Dónde estuviste ayer?
B: Ayer estuve en _____.

Places: el parque (=the park), el río (=the river), la montaña (=the mountain), la piscina (=the swimming pool), la finca (=the country house), el trabajo (=the workplace), la escuela (=the school), la Universidad (=the university), la casa (=the house), el dormitorio (=the dorm)

62.   Things you have to do

A: ¿Qué tienes que hacer más tarde?
B: Tengo que _____.

Verbs remain in the infinitive: hacer tarea (=to do homework), hacer deporte (=to do sports), hacer comida (=to make food), comprar comida (=to buy food), trabajar (=to work), cuidar los niños (=to take care of the children), estudiar (=to study), pagar cuentas (=to pay bills)

63.   Talk formally

Patrón: Buenas tardes.
Peón: Buenas tardes. ¿Cómo le va?
Patrón: Bien, muchas gracias, ¿y usted?
Peón: Muy bien, gracias.
Patrón: Necesito que usted me
            _____ (add action the
            master needs, using the subjunctive). Le voy a pagar
            _____ pesos.
Peón: No puedo _____ (add action in the
            infinitive) por _____ pesos.
Patrón: Si no lo hace (=if you don't do it), yo voy a
            _____ (add threat).

(Dialog continues arranging at least three types of work and three threats).
- Un dólar=cuatro mil pesos colombianos
- Verbs of work in the field: **recolectar** (to collect, to pich up), **cortar** (to cut), **abrir los surcos** (open the furrows), **arreglar el arado** (to fix the plow), **arreglar la cerca** (to fix the fence),

sembrar (to plant), **pintar el rancho** (to paint the ranch), **regar** (to water), **arriar las mulas** (to drive the mules).
- Produce: **papa** (potatoe), **maíz** (corn), **café** (coffee), **algodón** (cotton), **caña de azúcar** (sugar cane), **coca**
- Kettle: **vacas** (cows), **ovejas** (sheep),
- Verbs of threat: **contratar otro peón** (to hire another worker), **comprar su tierra muy barata** (buy his land very cheap), **sacar a su familia de la casa** (to expel his family from the house), **llamar al jefe paramilitar** (call the paramilitary boss), **desaparecer a sus hijos** (disappear his children)

With no subjunctive:

Patrón: Buenas tardes.
Peón: Buenas tardes. ¿Cómo está?
Patrón: Bien, muchas gracias, ¿y usted?
Peón: Muy bien, gracias.
Patrón: ¿Usted puede _____ (add verb of work with produce)? Pago (=I pay) _____ pesos.
Peón: No, no puedo _____ (add action in
the infinitive) por _____ pesos.
Patrón: Si no lo hace (=if you don't do it), yo voy a
_____ (add threat).

64.   Interview a politician

A=journalist, B=politician.

A: Buenas tardes, doctor/doctora _____.
B: Buenas tardes, señor/señora _____.
A: ¿Cuál es su plan para mejorar la educación?
B: Yo voy a _____ (add action + thing/people) y
_____ (add action + thing/people).
A: ¿Cuál es su plan para mejorar la salud (=health care)?
B: Yo voy a _____ (add action + thing/people) y
_____ (add action + thing/people).
A: ¿Cuál es su plan para mejorar la seguridad?
B: Yo voy a _____ (add action + thing/people) y
_____ (add action + thing/people).

A: ¿Cuál es su plan para mejorar la infraestructura?
B: Yo voy a _____ (add action + thing/people) y
_____ (add action + thing/people).

Actions: construir (build), dar dinero para (give money for),
contratar más (hire more…), mejorar la eficiencia de (improve the
efficiency of), controlar las finanzas de (control the finances of…),
hacer talleres para (to do workshops for)

Things: las escuelas (schools), los hospitales (hospitals), las
fuerzas armadas (army), las carreteras (roads), las calles (streets),
puentes (bridges)

People: profesores (teachers), médicos (doctors), enfermeras
(nurses), policías (police officers), militares (military officers)

A: ¿Cuál es su partido político?
B: Mi partido político es _____ (liberal o conservador?)
A: ¿Usted está de acuerdo con _____ *? (=Do you
agree with _____?)
B: Sí, estoy de acuerdo. / No, no estoy de acuerdo (your response
should be coherent with your party).
A: ¿Por qué?
B: Porque pienso que _____ (add a sentence in
Spanish).

*Add controversial topics in each question: 1) el aborto legal, 2)
matrimonio igualitario, 3) auxilios de desempleo, 4) vender tierras a
compañías de petróleo, 5) nacionalizar las compañías de petróleo,
6) privatizar los hospitales, 7) privatizar las escuelas, 8) aumentar
impuestos a los ricos, 9) mejorar auxilios de desempleo, 10) el
tratado de libre comercio con Estados Unidos, 11) dar dinero a los
campesinos.

A: ¿Alguna vez ha estado en la cárcel? (=Have you ever been in
jail?)
B: Sí, _____ (explain). / No, no
_____ (explain).
A: ¿Alguna vez le ha pegado a sus hijos? (=Have you ever beaten
your children?)

B: Sí, _____ (explain). / No, no
_____ (explain).
A: ¿Alguna vez ha recibido dinero del narcotráfico?
B: Sí, _____ (explain). / No, no
_____ (explain).
A: ¿Alguna vez ha estado en una pelea?
B: Sí, _____ (explain). / No, no
_____ (explain).
A: ¿Alguna vez ha tenido sexo con prostitutas?
B: Sí, _____ (explain). / No, no
_____ (explain).
A: ¿Alguna vez ha estado involucrado en un escándalo por
corrupción?
B: Sí, _____ (explain). / No, no
_____ (explain).

## 65.	Discuss a carnival in the past

A:Yo fui (=I went) al carnaval de negros y blancos. ¿Y tú?
B: Yo fui al carnaval de _____ (add carnival).
A: ¿Qué hiciste allí? (=What did you do there?)
B: Yo _____ (add the sentence from el
papelito you received). ¿Y tú?
A: Yo _____ .
Verbs: bailar bambuco, bailar huayno, beber chicha, salir con
amigos, tirar harina (=throw powder), jugar con los diablos, mirar el
desfile (=watch the parade), poner una máscara (**pus-** =put a
costume on), pintar la cara (=to paint the fase), llorar por la madre
tierra, hacer (**hic-**) bulla (=do noise)

Carnivals: Humahuaca (norte de Argentina), Negros y Blancos
(Pasto, Colombia), Barranquilla (norte de Colombia)

## 66.	Discuss exotic food – present perfect

A: **¿Has comido** _____?
B: **Sí, he comido** _____. **Comí** _____ (add
food, describe it). =Yes, I've eaten _____. I ate
_____.

No, nunca he comido _____. =No, I've never eaten
_____.

comida cruda=raw food, caimán=gator, cuy=guinea pig, tiburón=shark, piedras=rocks, venado=dear, papel=paper, tierra=soil

A: **¿Has bebido** _____?
B: **Sí, he bebido** _____. **Bebí** _____ (add drink, describe it). =*Yes, I've eaten* _____. *I ate* _____.
No, nunca he bebido _____. =*No, I've never eaten* _____.

sangre humana=human blood, orina=urine, jabón líquido=liquid soap, alcohol=alcohol, agua de lluvia=rain water

67.   Things you do when you arrive home

A: Cuando llegas a tu cuarto, ¿qué música _____? (=oír)
B: Yo _____ _____ (add verb and type of music).
A: Cuando llegas a tu cuarto, ¿dónde _____ tus medias? (=poner)
B: Yo _____ mis medias en _____.
A: Cuando llegas a tu cuarto, ¿cuánto dinero _____? (=traer)
B: Yo _____ _____ (add money).
A: Cuando llegas a tu cuarto, ¿qué le _____ al espejo? (=decir)
B: Yo le _____ _____ (add thing you say).
A: Cuando llegas a tu cuarto, ¿quién _____ contigo? (=venir)
B: _____ (add person, or **nadie**) _____ conmigo.

- **Hacer**: hago, haces, hace, hacemos, hacen
- **Poner**: pongo, pones, pone, ponemos, ponen
- **Oír**: oigo, oyes, oye, oímos, oyen
- **Decir**: digo, dices, dice, decimos, dicen
- **Traer**: traigo, traes, trae, traemos, traen
- **Venir**: vengo, vienes, viene, venimos, vienen
- **Tener**: tengo, tienes, tienen, tenemos, tienen

68.   Command someone do something

Take the yo-form and change the vowel to make the subjunctive:
hacer – hag**o** – hag**a**
poner – pong**o** – _____

empezar (=to start) - empiezo - _____

contar (=to tell) - cuento - _____

oír – oigo – _____

dormir – duermo – _____

jugar - juego - _____

seguir (=to continue) - sigo - _____

revolver (=to stir) – revuelvo - _____

echar (=to pour) – echo - _____

decir (=to say) – digo - _____

venir (=to come) – vengo - _____

69.   State a recipe

Organize in order by adding numbers 1-11 on how to make arepa colombiana, and state the recipe by using the singular formal command.

- Agregar el queso (_____)
- Lavarse las manos (_____)
- Echar (=pour) la harina (_____)
- Asar la arepa (_____)
- Revolver la harina (_____)
- Traer el agua (_____)
- Hacer una masa (_____)
- Hacer una bolita (_____)
- Aplastar (=flatten) la bolita (_____)
- Agregar la sal (_____)
- Prender la estufa (=stove) (_____)

70.   Give directions, formal

A: Disculpe, señor OR señora.

B: Sí, dígame. (Yes, tell me).

A: ¿Cómo llego a _____? (=how do I arrive to, add place)

B: _____ (=provides directions)

siga derecho = go straight, gire a la derecha = turn right, gire a la izquierda = turn left, un poquito = a little bit, de un paso = give a step

71.   Give directions, informal

A: Disculpa.

B: Sí, dime. (Yes, tell me).

A: ¿Cómo llego a _____? (=how do I arrive to, add place)
B: _____ (=provides directions)
sigue derecho = go straight, **gira a la derecha** = turn right, **gira a la izquierda** = turn left, **un poquito** = a little bit, **da un paso** = give a step

72. Directions and offer to help talk

A: Disculpe, señor OR señora.
B: Sí, dígame (Yes, let me know).
A: ¿Cómo llego a _____? (=how do I arrive to, add place)
B: _____ (=provides directions)
A: No entiendo (=I don't understand).
B: ¿Quiere que **lo** (if hearer is male), **la** (if hearer is female) acompañe (=subjunctive)?
A: Sí, gracias.
B: ¿Qué necesita hacer allá? (=What do you need to do there?
A: Necesito _____ (make up something you need to do in that place).

siga derecho = go straight, gire a la derecha = turn right, gire a la izquierda = turn left.

Destinations: el baño (=the bathroom), el salón # _____, el salón # _____, el bebedero (=the water fountain), la máquina vendedora (=the vending machine), la fotocopiadora (=copy machine), el parqueadero (=the parking lot), la puerta principal (=the main door), el teatro (=the theater)

73. Story of friendship break-up

Tell the story of a someone who was a good friend of you, and who is not your friend anymore.
Yo tenía un amigo que se llamaba _____.
Él OR ella era _____, _____ y _____ (add qualities), pero era _____ y _____ (add defects).

Un día (=one day), Él OR ella _____ (add in preterit something did person did wrong). Por eso, ya no hablamos más. (For that, we don' speak any more).

Continue telling the story on how the friendship ended.

74.   Negotiate chores

Before starting, announce who you are, and your role:
A: Soy _____ y soy esposo/esposa.
B: Soy _____ y soy esposo/esposa.
Then show your negotiation by picking verbs:
A: Tú vas a _____. Yo voy a _____.
B: No, tú vas a _____. Yo voy a _____.
A: No, tú vas a _____. Yo voy a _____.
B: No, tú vas a _____. Yo voy a _____.
A: No, tú vas a _____. Yo voy a _____.
B: No, tú vas a _____. Yo voy a _____.

Verbs: cocinar (=to cook), limpiar (=to clean), tomar chicha (=drink chicha), comer cuy (=to eat guinnea pig), tomar té de coca (=to drink coca tea), llevar a los niños a la escuela (=to take children to school), hacer deporte (=to do sports), montar bicicleta (=to ride bikes), trabajar en construcción (=to work in construction), dormir (=to sleep), leer (=to read), cuidar al bebé (=to take care of the baby), alimentar al bebé (=to feed the baby).

Change the dialog using formal command:
A: Cocine que yo voy a comer.
B: No, señor, USTED _____ que yo voy a _____.
A: No, señora, USTED _____ que yo voy a _____.
B: No, señor, USTED _____ que yo voy a _____.
A: No, señora, USTED _____ que yo voy a _____.
B: No, señor, USTED _____ que yo voy a _____.

75.   Epílogo

You can cover the present, past, and future in just three Spanish lessons. Most conversations in any language revolve around the I and You forms because most speakers talk about themselves. By learning I/You, you'll be able to hold fluent conversations, build confidence, and lay the foundation to talk about he/she. The he/she forms are mainly used for storytelling and gossip, and once you start using them, you'll know you're well on your way to being integrated into the community and won't need extra lessons.

Traditional language methods rely on a generative approach. They focus on teaching you a core set of patterns that create countless combinations of verbs, nouns, and words. While it's important to learn all of this and try to understand the big picture of learning Spanish, it's not the most efficient way to actually use Spanish in conversation.

My approach adopts a functionalist perspective. This view suggests that language is not unlimited and that people tend to say the same thing again and again. Although many possibilities exist, people usually speak in small, patterned chunks rather than being highly creative or elaborate. In terms of language learning, this approach means you can achieve conversational proficiency in any language by mastering common dialogue chunks. Tourist guides often use such methods. However, some generativist comments will help you understand the chunks you're practicing and provide a foundation to keep working on your own.

This workbook combines a functionalist with a task-based approach. That means it starts by giving you a brief communicative task to complete (greet, discuss, tell, respond), along with a fixed template in Spanish that you can fill out with vocabulary and some minor conjugation changes. Trying Spanish will connect you with a vibrant culture and community, while also opening new horizons for your neurocognitive system. You can use this book with any native Spanish speaker, regardless of their teaching experience, to lead your own educational journey.

www.ingramcontent.com/pod-product-compliance
Lightning Source LLC
Chambersburg PA
CBHW070050040426
42331CB00034B/2960